THE BIG BOOK OF THE DARK

Written by Helena Haraštová

Illustrated by Jiří Franta

BOOK HOUSE
a SALARIYA imprint

What is Darkness?

Let there be light...

What is darkness?

Life on Earth would be impossible without sunlight. Yet sometimes light disappears and darkness falls. Darkness is simply the absence of light. Light never goes away completely, but when there is very little of it the human eye does not perceive it – but the eyes of some creatures, like cats, do. Therefore cats and other beasts see better in the dark than we do.

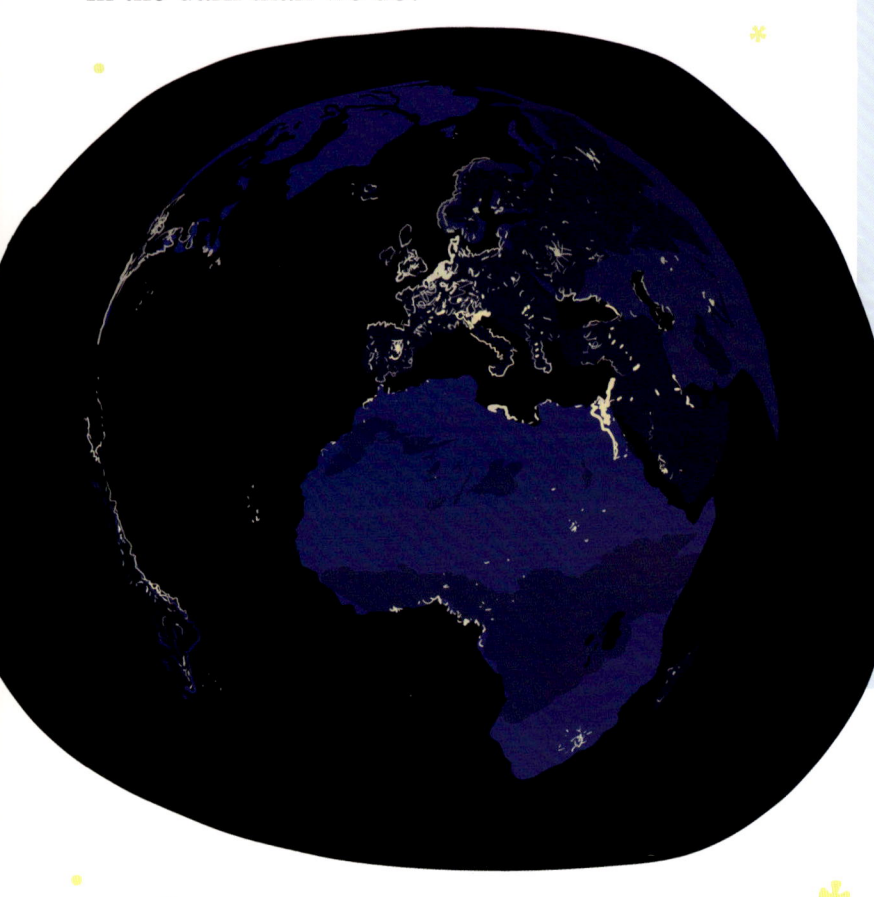

Earth at night

When astronauts look at our planet from space at night, they can see a lot of lights shining on its surface. Large cities produce so much light at night that it penetrates the Earth's atmosphere and is visible from space.

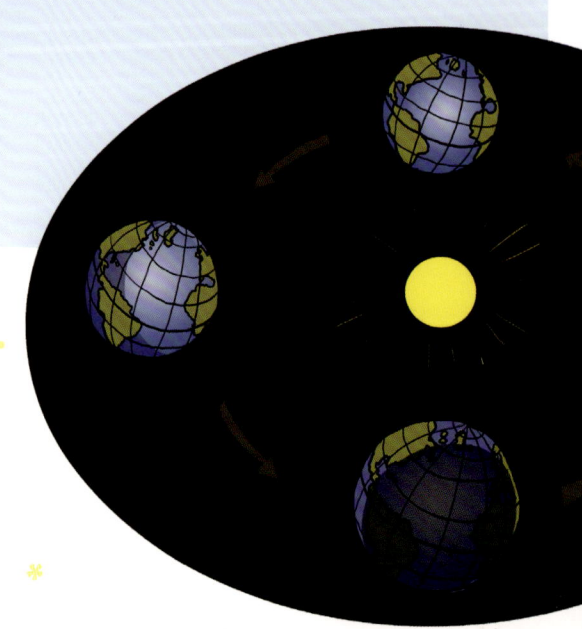

What is light?

What is darkness and what is light? Do scary creatures live in the dark? People have always asked such questions. The ancient Greeks thought that light was transmitted by the human eye in the same way that torchlight works. Today we know that the light we see comes from an enormous star in the centre of our galaxy – the Sun. The rays of the Sun travel an unbelievable 149,600,000 kilometres to reach the Earth in just 8 minutes! Some of the Sun's light is invisible to us, but certain scientific instruments can pick it up, as do some animals.

Plato

When night falls

Does the Sun simply disappear from the sky at night? No, it stays exactly where it is. Our planet constantly rotates around its own axis. As the planet turns, so do we: sometimes we face the Sun but by night-time we have turned away from its light. Every place on Earth finds itself in sunlight for part of the day only. When it is night where we are, it is daytime on the other side of the world. Draw a small face on a ball and aim torchlight on it. Now turn the ball slowly around its axis. Can you see how the drawing is sometimes bathed in light and sometimes lost in shadow?

Sources of artificial light

Our ancestors were afraid of the dark because thieves, ghosts and dangerous animals might be hiding in it. To protect themselves from these real and imaginary foes, they discovered and later invented various sources of light. This allowed them to carry on after nightfall.

Fire

In prehistoric times hunters realised that fire was not only a source of light but also heat. The first fires resulted from lightning strikes, but people soon learned to start fires using flint or twigs and strips of bark.

Torch

Before long, people learned to carry fire with them. They used two kinds of torches – a dried log fixed to a post or a lighted bar soaked in pitch or oil. Soldiers used them when on long night-time marches. Indoors, open fires were very dangerous.

Oil lamp

Oil lamps could burn for several hours, and they were safer than fiery torches. The wicks were made from small pieces of wood and were placed in small bowls of rapeseed or olive oil. Oil lamps were made of stone, ceramics, metal, or even glass.

Candle

In the Middle Ages, poor people used candles made of tallow, and also of fish or whale oil, which had a strong smell. Only the rich could afford the luxury of wax candles. People made notches on candles as a rough way to measure time gradually 'burning' away.

Kerosene lamp

The kerosene lamp was invented in the mid 19th century. Light was created by burning kerosene, a type of oil. Kerosene lamps had a fuel tank, a wick, a glass chimney that made the light stronger, and a mirror to reflect more light.

Light bulb

The light bulb was designed in 1879 by the American Thomas Edison, whose first bulb burned for about 40 hours. Today's bulbs can last for months or even years. The filament inside does not burn down, as the glass bulb contains no air.

Modern sources of light

The invention of the light bulb led to the invention of reflectors, fluorescent lamps, and even giant illuminated billboards. Today's city centres are lit night and day by many luminous advertisements, and roads are lined with streetlamps.

Nature and darkness

The forest never sleeps.

Field cricket

Male field crickets chirp loudly at night to attract females and to mark their territory. They produce this sound by rubbing their wings together.

Greater mouse-eared bat

Although bats are mammals, they can fly. They sleep by day and hunt by night. They have learned to emit ultrasonic signals or high-pitched sounds that are inaudible to humans. These signals bounce back off objects in their path to inform them of any obstacles. This process of navigation is called echolocation.

Grey wolf

Wolves live in organized packs that hunt together to attack much bigger animals like deer and cattle. Their sense of smell allows them to track their prey from 3 kilometres away! Wolves howl, not at the moon but to call the pack to the hunt or to warn of danger.

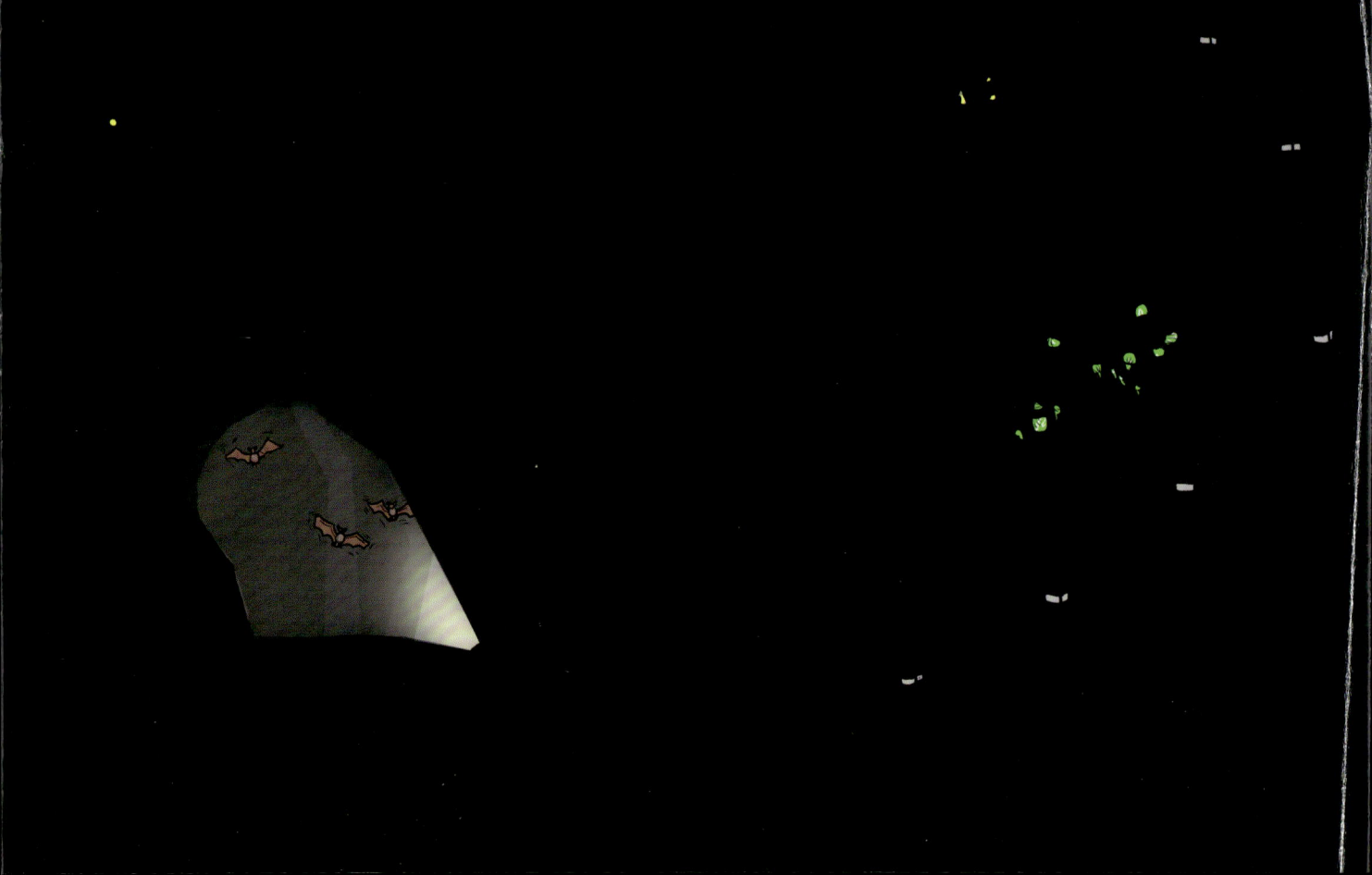

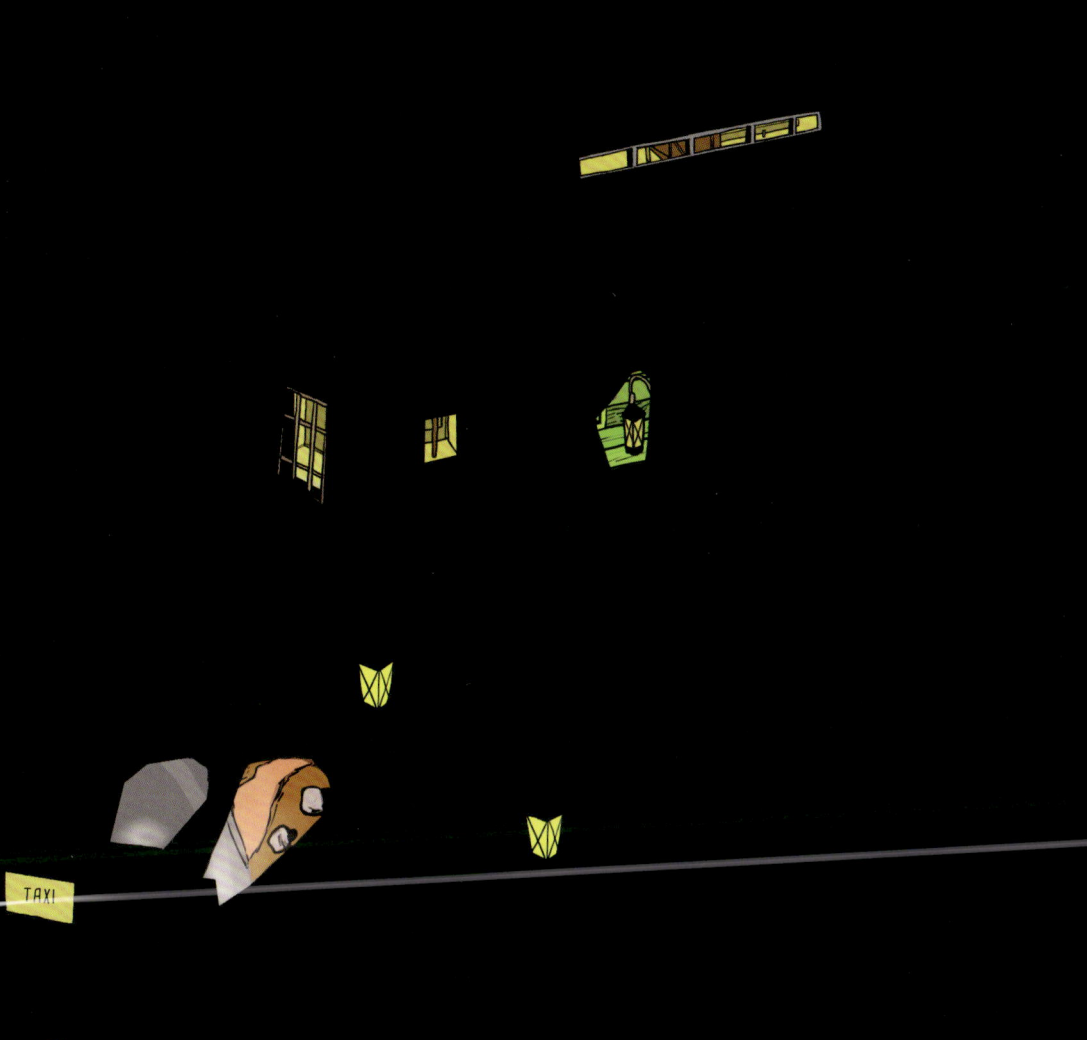

Death's-head hawkmoth

Butterflies of the night are known as moths. The death's-head hawkmoth owes its intimidating name to skull-shaped markings between its wings. These moths fly south to Africa for the winter. In spring, their offspring return to Europe.

Common nightingale

The nightingale can sing beautifully for hours without repeating a single melody. It can be heard during the day and at night.

Common frog

The night-time croaking of frogs may keep you awake, but for frogs it is very important. It is the song by which the male woos the female.

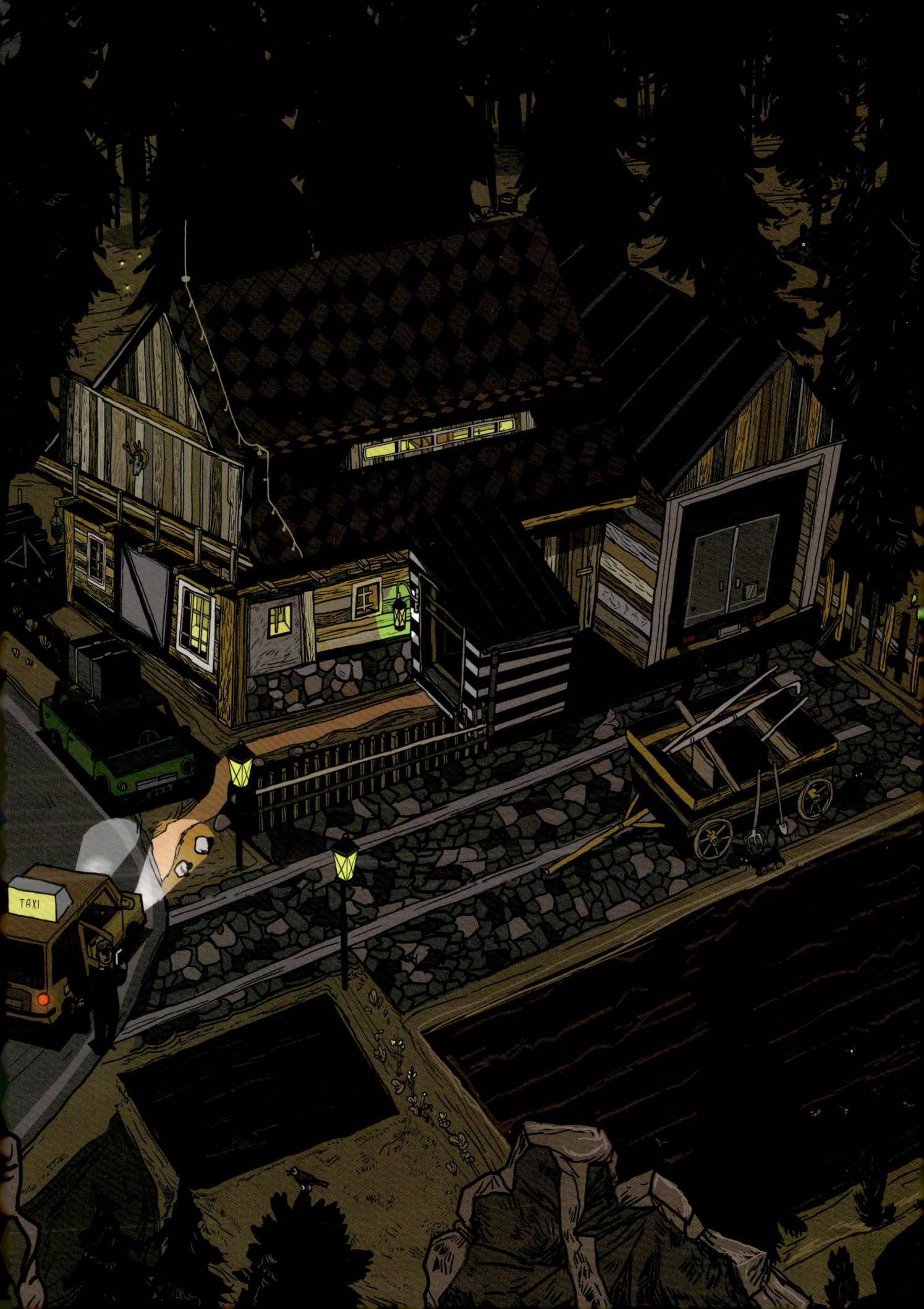

Nature and darkness

wildcat

The wildcat is a close relative of the domestic cat. It hunts at night so its eyes and ears are adapted for this purpose. It can spot a small bird, mouse or vole from a distance of 100 metres – the length of a football pitch!

European hedgehog

When outdoors at night-time have you ever heard strange stomping and snorting noises? Fear not – you are probably close to a hedgehog. At night, this small mammal hunts insects and earthworms with its excellent sense of smell. When in danger, a hedgehog rolls itself into a prickly ball.

How plants grow

During the day, plants focus mainly on the processes of photosynthesis and flowering rather than growing. But at night they grow amazingly fast – check this out with plants you grow at home.

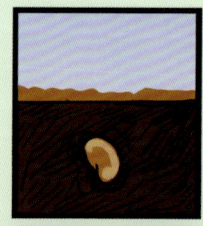

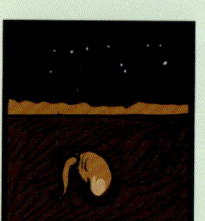

Eurasian eagle owl

The Eurasian eagle owl is an outstanding hunter. It has enormous eyes to see at night as well as by day. It also has excellent hearing, as its soft wing feathers make very little sound as it flies. It commonly feeds on hedgehogs, although it is also capable of bringing down a young roe deer.

Evening primrose

Some exotic plants bloom at night; these include orchid species and certain field and forest herbs. Evening primrose can grow to be 2 metres tall. Its flowers open around six in the evening and are pollinated by moths at dawn. They wither and fall off during the day.

Common glow-worm

Glow-worms are among the most remarkable inhabitants of the night-time landscape. They emit a bright green light that switches on and off depending on their needs. Females light up while waiting in the grass and the males when in flight. This makes it easier for them to find each other.

Bitter oyster

During the day, the bitter oyster looks just like an ordinary mushroom. It grows in clusters on the trunks of living or dead deciduous trees. At night, it miraculously lights up and emits green light thanks to a special compound in its body.

How do plants breathe?

If the changing pattern of day and night were to end, most of the world's plants would die, resulting in the extinction of practically all life on Earth. By day, plants absorb food in the form of sugar, and release oxygen into the atmosphere. This oxygen is breathed by animals and humans and the process is known as photosynthesis. At night, plants take in oxygen and release carbon dioxide. It is thanks to photosynthesis that we have enough oxygen on Earth.

The dark, deep ocean

Life in eternal darkness.

The deep ocean is forever dark. The great mass of water creates an enormous pressure and the temperature there never gets above 4 degrees Celsius. The creatures that live in these adverse conditions are very special. So far we know about 5,700 animal species that live deep in the ocean, though there are probably many more.

Bioluminescent plankton

Plankton are small animals and plants that live on the surface of seas and oceans. Plankton of the species *noctiluca scintillans* glow magnificently in the dark.

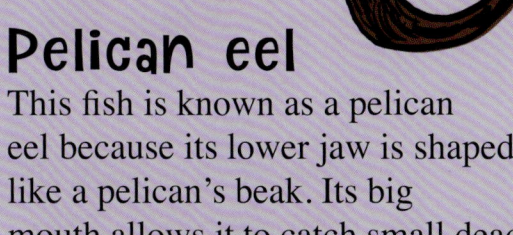

Pelican eel

This fish is known as a pelican eel because its lower jaw is shaped like a pelican's beak. Its big mouth allows it to catch small dead creatures that fall to the seabed.

Black dragonfish

A black dragonfish female is a real terror of the deep. It is about 40 centimetres long, and has a mouth full of sharp, transparent, fang-like teeth. Under the chin is a protuberance with a ball on the end that glows in the dark. It feeds on other fish. Males are smaller and have neither teeth nor a luminescent ball. It is very clear who is the head of a dragonfish family.

Laying eggs

Sea turtles are perfectly equipped for life in the sea: they swim quickly and can remain underwater for a long time without having to breathe. Once every two or three years, females return at night to the beach where they were born. Here they lay their eggs in the sand. They bury about 100 eggs at a depth of one metre before returning to the sea. Small turtles that hatch from the eggs instinctively follow the light of the Moon to head straight for the sea.

Eternal darkness

Sunlight only penetrates up to 1 kilometre below sea level. This means that creatures that live deeper than this are in absolute darkness. Often darkness can begin only 200 metres below the surface.

Giant squid

The squid is a giant of the deep ocean. With its tentacles outstretched this predator is an unbelievable 18 metres long. Its eyes are 30 centimetres in diameter! It is an active hunter.

The dark, deep ocean

Black smokers and white smokers

Black smokers and white smokers are enormous undersea chimney structures that are found on the ocean bed. They are created by undersea volcanoes that spew molten metals from the depths of our planet. Even here there is life, such as the pink lizardfish and the Hoff crab.

Jellyfish

The *aequorea* species of jellyfish light up at night to intimidate their enemies. They live off the coast of North America.

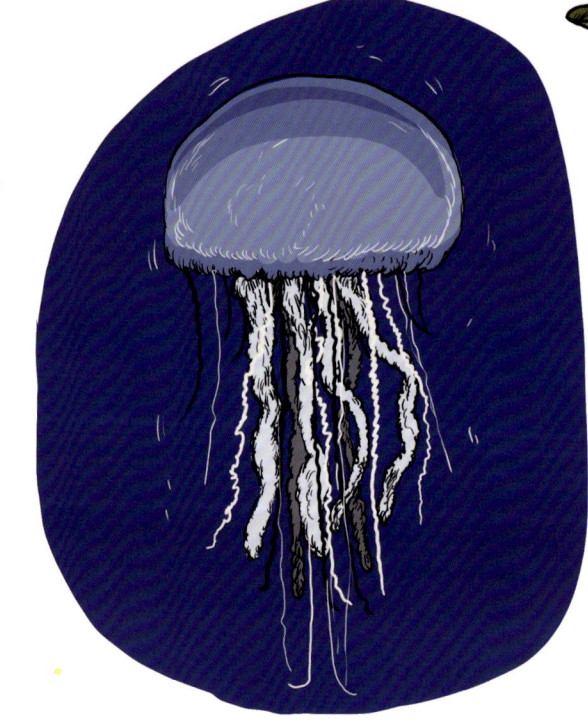

The deepest place on Earth

The Mariana Trench is the deepest place on Earth, at 11 kilometres below sea level. It is at the bottom of the Atlantic Ocean. Even here, there is life.

Black seadevil

The black seadevil is a species of angler fish. It has spines instead of fins and many long, sharp teeth in its wide mouth. Like the black dragonfish, it has a luminescent ball on the front of its head. This attracts curious prey and also scares away its enemies.

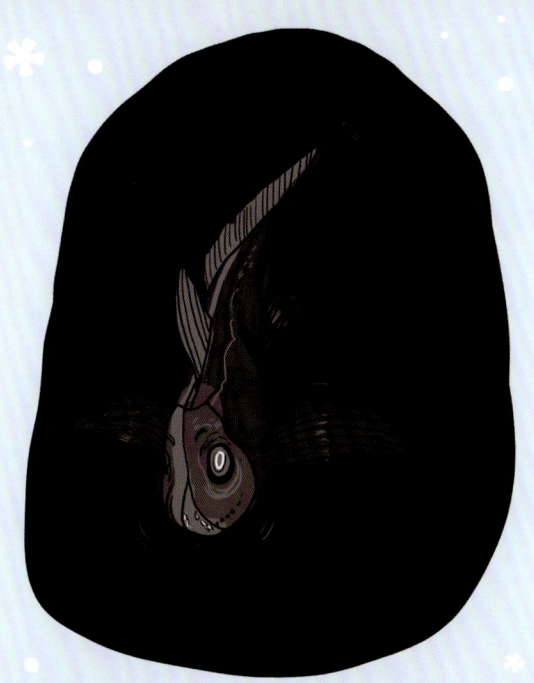

Coelacanth

Scientists long believed that the coelacanth became extinct in prehistoric times. Then, in 1938, it was discovered by chance! This 'living fossil' is about 1.5 metres long. It usually hovers sluggishly above the seabed but it attacks its prey surprisingly fast.

Holocephali

Although most species of Holocephali are long extinct, some still exist about 200 metres below sea level. These cartilaginous fish have scaleless skin and two dorsal fins.

Cuttlefish

The cuttlefish is about 1.5 metres long, and it is a very intelligent creature. It waits patiently on the seabed for its prey, approaching it slowly and subtly. As soon as it is close enough, it grabs the prey with its two long tentacles. A cuttlefish can also change colour to match its surroundings. When in danger it releases a cloud of dark ink and disappears into it.

Transport and darkness

Transport doesn't stop at night.

An international airport never sleeps. So many people fly away on holiday, to see relatives or on business that many planes take off or land at night. Airport staff work through the night.

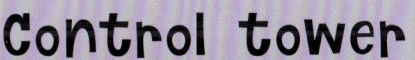

Arrivals hall

On arrival in a foreign country, your travel documents are checked before you can collect your luggage. Each flight is assigned a particular conveyor belt so that passengers from different parts of the world can find their suitcases easily.

Control tower

Air traffic controllers in the control tower direct the comings and goings of all aeroplanes. They know how each runway is currently occupied and the schedule of all flights. Without air traffic controllers, aeroplanes wouldn't be able to land and take off safely. They are the most important people at the airport!

Terminals

Before you depart from an airport you must find the check-in desk, show your passport, hand in your luggage and receive a boarding pass. A metal detector checks your suitcase for any suspicious items while an X-ray scanner checks the contents of your hand luggage. Then you have time to shop or eat. As your departure time nears, you go to the gate assigned for your flight. Flight attendants will soon guide you onto the aeroplane.

Hangars

Out-of-service aeroplanes rest in airport hangars. These spacious halls have very wide doors to accommodate a plane's wingspan.

Airport records

The world's first airport was built for military use during the First World War. The first civilian airport was opened in Germany in 1922. The world's largest airport is in Atlanta, USA. But the city that serves most passengers is London, which has five airports.

Transport and darkness

Fuel depots

If fuel were to run out, aeroplanes wouldn't get very far. It is stored in vast tanks not far from the airport. Because fuel is combustible and explosive, no one is allowed in the depot without a permit.

Roadways and runways

An airport covers a huge area that is made up of roadways for airport vehicles and runways for planes to land and take off from. Other runways are used to move planes to and from hangars. All movements are strictly managed by the airport as pilots must know which they can use at any given moment, so as to avoid collisions.

Station

A large international airport often has its own fully-staffed train station, equipped with a ticket office, a newsagent and a lost-property office. Many people use the train rather than a bus service or their own car, as trains don't get stuck in traffic jams.

Conductor, dispatcher, pointsman

pointsman

conductors

dispatcher

A conductor works on a train. He is responsible for the safety and comfort of the passengers, checks their tickets and can give them advice. A dispatcher signals each train driver using a hand-held sign that is green on one side and red on the other. The green side gives the signal for the train to pull out, while the red one instructs it to stop. A pointsman operates a device called a point where the track divides into two parts. He can change the direction in which the train will continue its journey.

Lost property

People in a hurry often lose personal belongings, luggage or documents at the station. With luck, any such items are handed in to the lost-property office, where the original owner may claim them back.

Darkness and the city

Many people work while you sleep!

Cities, too, are wakeful at night. The street lamps come on, the traffic subsides and the streets gradually empty. However, there are places that remain busy throughout the night, such as hospitals, restaurants, theatres, hotels and newspaper offices.

Police

Police officers must be equally alert by day and night. Those working the night shift have to cope with crimes committed under cover of darkness as well as making sure people are safe. Walkie-talkies help them to respond to emergency calls immediately.

Ambulance

After a serious accident, the injured person is taken in an ambulance to hospital, where doctors and nurses are waiting to offer immediate help.

Accident and Emergency

Although normal hospital consulting rooms close in the early evening, help remains on hand for people who get into accidents after that. Urgent cases are seen by Accident and Emergency, which treats patients without appointments.

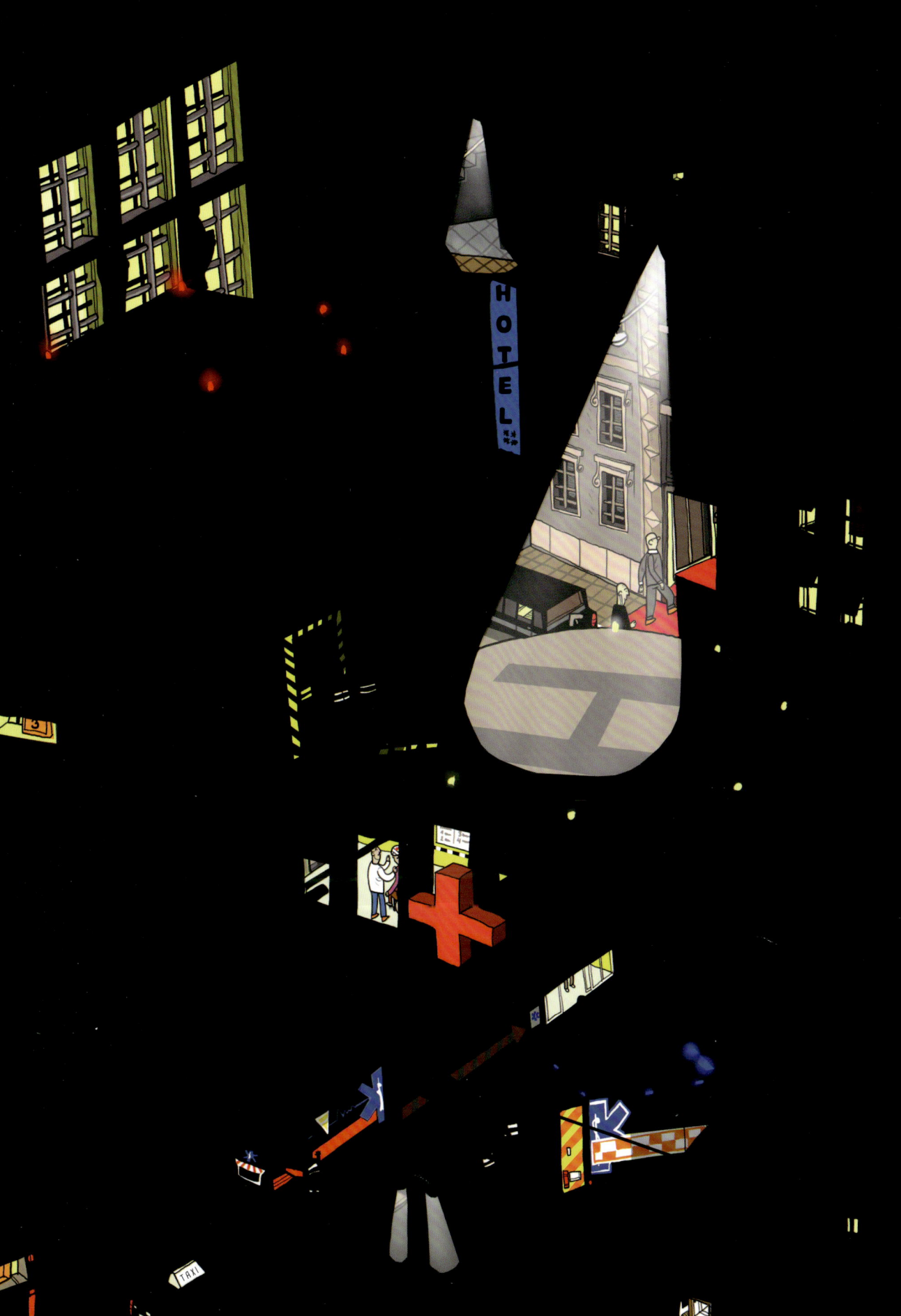

Intensive care

In an Intensive Care Unit doctors and nurses provide constant care for people whose lives are in danger, perhaps as a result of a traffic accident, burns or other serious injury. These units are small with only a few beds, equipped with the most up-to-date equipment.

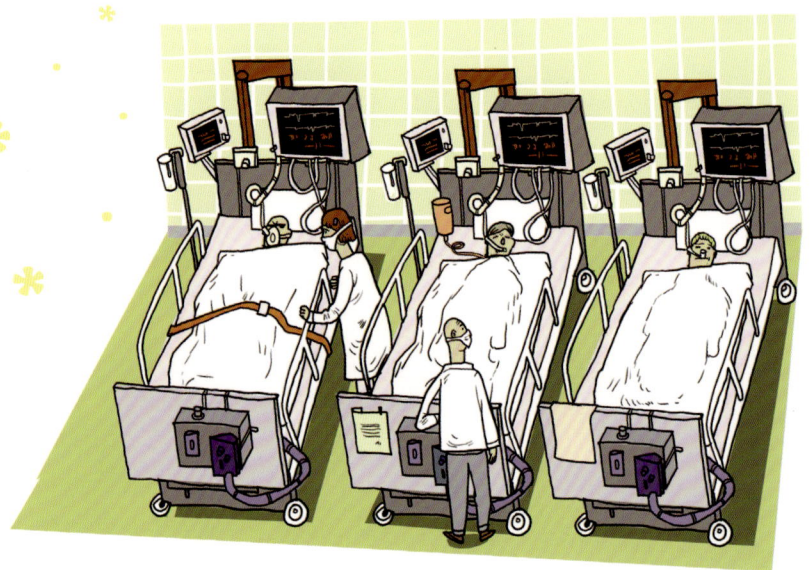

Surgery

Doctors perform operations in the hospital theatre. If a patient's life is in danger, it may be necessary to operate in the middle of the night. Some operations – on the heart or brain, for example – can last several hours and are very demanding.

Heliport

If it is too difficult for an ambulance to reach a patient in time, the hospital sends a rescue helicopter. On returning with the patient, it lands on the roof of the hospital on an illuminated landing pad known as a heliport. Here doctors and nurses await the patient, ready to transport him/her to the nearest operating theatre, where life-saving surgery can be performed.

Darkness and the city

Red fox

The fox's natural habitat is in woodlands but many live in cities, too. At dusk and dawn they hunt for birds and rodents to eat. Sometimes they feed on the rubbish found in and around dustbins.

Night buses

Although at night there is less demand for public transport as most people are asleep, transport companies do operate a limited service of buses and trams.

Hotel

Hotel staff often have a lot of work to do at night tending to their guests. People often check in late at night while others may dine late or relax in the hotel bar into the early hours of the morning. The night clerk keeps track of people arriving and leaving the hotel and is responsible for the safety of all guests.

Theatre

In the evening, people like to go to the theatre. Whether the play is a comedy or tragedy, there are many people working behind the scenes as well as the actors on the stage. But when the curtain falls this is not the end of the evening's work at the theatre. As the spectators hurry home, the make-up artists remove the actors' make-up and wigs, the dressers collect the costumes, props are stored and the theatre is made ready for tomorrow's performance. Actors often meet up again after the performance to relax.

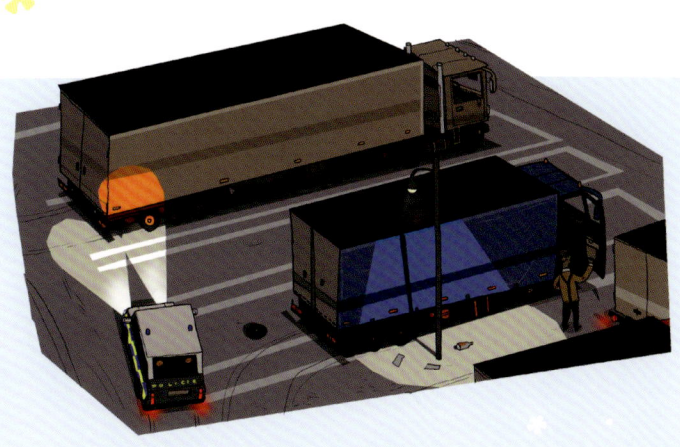

Parked trucks

Driving trucks that transport goods long distances can be very exhausting! While some truck drivers sleep over in motels at night, others sleep in their vehicles, which they park off the roadside to keep them out of the way of other traffic.

Newspaper office and printing house

Every morning newsagents sell the latest editions of the newspapers. To create a newspaper, its staff have to work on their articles, photographs and the overall appearance of the newspaper through the night. Meanwhile, the printing house prepares to produce copies of the newspaper; before sunrise the printer hands these over to drivers who will deliver bundles of newspapers all over the city.

21

Darkness and the village

A village at night is also full of life!

Nightwatchman

Long ago, nightwatchmen would patrol villages and towns, as it was their job to protect houses and their occupants from thieves, enemies and fire. A nightwatchman carried a handgun for protection and a horn that he would blow to warn people of any danger.

Night sky and constellations of the winter sky

The next time you find yourself in the countryside, don't forget to take a good look at the sky. You will see thousands of stars that you cannot see in town because the streetlights there create too much light. Did you know that the sky's constellations move with the seasons? In winter the constellation we see most clearly is Orion.

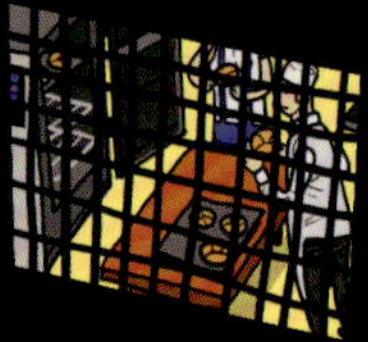

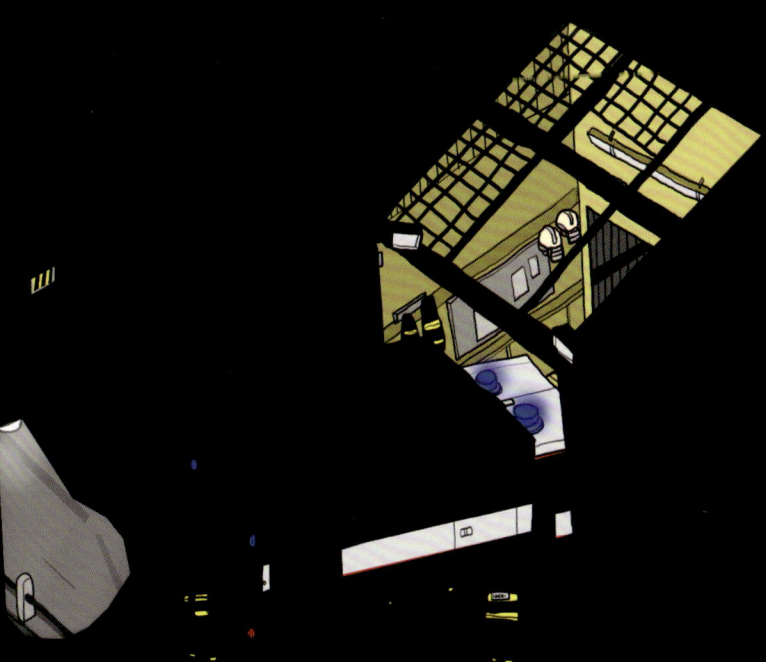

Volunteer firefighters

Many villages have a volunteer fire brigade made up of brave people who are prepared to rush to the aid of neighbours in case of fire, flooding or other dangers. These firefighters are greatly respected. They have to be ready to act in the middle of the night.

European pine marten

The marten may be small, but it is a very nimble and cunning animal. At night it hunts birds and small animals, often coming close to people's houses, especially if they keep hens. It has excellent hearing and sight. You are unlikely to see it by day, when it hides in the hollows of trees and abandoned nests.

European mole

Earthworms aren't the only creatures that live underground in the dark – moles do, too. They have eyes, but their sight is very poor, so they rely mostly on their sense of smell and their hearing. They dig tunnels with their spade-like paws and hunt insects, larvae, frogs, worms and mice. They can eat their own weight in food in just one day!

Darkness and the village

Dark hour

In the past, before electricity had reached villages, people often observed a 'dark hour' after nightfall. The work done, the whole family would get together in a candlelit room to tell thrilling stories, which the children would listen to with bated breath. Why don't you try a 'dark hour'? One evening, ask your parents to switch off the lights, light a candle, sit around the table and tell each other scary stories. You'll see what great fun it is!

Cowshed and barn

The cows, goats, sheep and pigs that country people ke also like to sleep at night. Soft hay makes a wonderfu bed for the animals and each morning, often before sunrise, the farmer comes feed them and lead them o to pasture. Some animals, however, live in large facto farms and never get out int the meadow.

Earthworm

The darkness underground is absolute, yet there is life there. Earthworms are small, thin creatures that live in the ground. They make tunnels that create corridors of air that help to make the soil fertile. Earthworms do not need to see – if they find themselves in daylight they sense danger and quickly burrow underground again. The body of the exotic *eisenia lucens* earthworm produces a luminous slime. In winter, earthworms sleep day and night underground, waiting for the spring to come.

Bakery

A baker makes bread, rolls, cakes and other baked products. For all these delicious things to be fresh in the shops each morning, he has to work through the night. Although today a lot of this work can be done with machines, without the baker's skill and experience his products wouldn't taste half as good.

Moon

Over the moon!

What is the Moon?

The Moon is neither a star nor a planet; it is Earth's only natural satellite, which means that it has orbited our planet for millions of years. The Moon is round and it is many times smaller than the Earth. When we look at the sky, we see only half of the Moon; the other half is always hidden from view. Until scientists learned how to send space probes to the Moon, we had no idea what its dark side looked like. Now we know that it is not so different from the side we can already see.

Does the Moon shine?

It seems to us that the Moon shines at night, but this is actually an illusion. The Moon has no light of its own – it reflects the light of the Sun.

Many forms of the Moon

The Moon takes 28 days to travel all the way around the Earth. The Sun illuminates different parts of the Moon depending on each stage of its orbit. When the whole moon is lit, we call this a full moon, and describe a crescent moon as waxing or waning.

Getting to know the Moon

At night, astronomers can observe the surface of the Moon closely through a telescope and we can dream of one day being up there ourselves. The first humans to walk on the Moon were the Americans Neil Armstrong and Buzz Aldrin in 1969. Even today it is extremely expensive to fly there.

Glossary

Ancient Greeks
People who lived in Greece two thousand years ago and built a civilisation that changed Western culture forever.

Perceive
To see or understand something.

Plato
An ancient Greek philosopher who believed that people could see by emitting light from their eyes.

Pollination
How plants are able to reproduce: by having their seeds transferred from their male to their female organs by insects, animals or wind.

Protuberance
Something that sticks out from something else.

Tentacle
A flexible, thin limb some animals have and use to grab things or move around.

Thomas Edison
An American inventor and businessman who developed many important devices, such as the light bulb and the motion picture camera.

Index

Published in Great Britain in MMXVII by
Book House, an imprint of
The Salariya Book Company Ltd
25 Marlborough Place, Brighton BN1 1UB
www.salariya.com

ISBN: 978-1-911242-99-4

SALARIYA

1 3 5 7 9 8 6 4 2

© Designed by B4U Publishing, 2016
A member of Albatros Media Group
Author: Helena Haraštová
Illustrations: Jiří Franta
www.b4upublishing.com
All rights reserved.
Translation rights arranged though JNJ Agency, Texas Allen
English text © The Salariya Book Company Ltd MMXVII